THERE IS A TREASURE IN YOU

Daramola Joel Odunayo

Tel: 08033275896, 07028206482

ISBN: 9798370013430

Published by

CHRIST THE REDEEMER'S MINISTRIES

1-9, Redemption Way, P.M.B. 1088, Ebute Metta, Lagos, Nigeria.

Unless otherwise stated, all scriptural quotation are from the Authorized King James Version of the Holy Bible.

Printed in Nigeria by: **CRM PRESS**

KM 46 Lagos-Ibadan Expressway, CRM Shopping Complex,

Back of Old Auditorium, Redemption Camp,

Tel: 08077833792, 08069452037

E-mail: crmpress@yahoo.com

TABLE OF CONTENT

DEDICATION

This book is dedicated to our Lord Jesus Christ; my Saviour and the Holy Spirit, my senior partner in life and ministry and my heavenly Father, the Almighty God (YAHWEH) and to my biological father, Late Pa Solomon Kolawole Daramola, also to everyone that attends 'Power Service' our weekly breakthrough and deliverance service in various locations.

ACKNOWLEDGEMENT

I appreciate the efforts of everybody who at different stages contributed immensely to the success of this book. First to my better half who helped me in typing the book, Pastor Mrs. C.O. Daramola, and for her selfless effort at reading the manuscript and making very useful adjustment – much love; also to Pastor Aremu of CRM Press who helped in proofreading, and many others who helped to bring the dream to reality. God bless you all.

Nothing was ever built to be useless. Only man makes a thing useless. The carbon dioxide that man breath out is useful for the plants to breath in, while the oxygen that man breath in was the exhale of plants!

Man has to invest judiciously finding His space to understand His pace; those were the words imprinted in this work. Read it! Its Life! -

Daniel Olawande (P.Daniel)

INTRODUCTION

THE HIDDEN POTENTIALS INSIDE YOU

"And God is able to make all grace abound toward you; that ye, always having all sufficiency in all things, may abound to every good work." (2 Corinthians 9:8)

I am holding two bags of Lipton tea – a brand of tea popular in my country Nigeria and some other parts of the world; one is dipped in hot water while the other one is lying on my palm. The one on my palm is still nice, fresh, well packaged and its potential is still untapped. The one inside the hot water now looks rough having been dipped inside the hot water, but it is finding expression being diffused in the water; thus, it is fulfilling a purpose. The hot water aided the process of its usefulness so that the addition of either sugar and milk, or lime or whatever is needed (according to individual's preference) can bring satisfactory taste.

Friends, the underlining factor of a potential being realized is the process of its transformation from being potent to being kinetic (functional and profiting), from being reserved to being used, hence the illustration of the hot water making the tea bag drinkable.

This is the case with the human brain. The more it is used, the better it functions. To use it, you engage in activities that will keep it working – such as strategic thinking, reading for information, researching, analysis, critical thinking, and the likes.

Come to think of it. God did not create stools, or a house, or a chair, He simply created the raw materials for making them. To make them, He gave man the gift of His brain. With that, the human race now witness the excellent innovations, inventions, creativity and different wonderful creations of man by just engaging his brain. That is an example of the potential that God has given to man. You use it, you enjoy it.

I need to also say that you are created a gift to the world. For you to be useful, you have to discover what you are meant to fulfill and what is kept inside you.

The hard times and situations, trials, temptations and afflictions constitute the proverbial 'hot water' we all must pass through before our potentials can be realized. Consequently, we become useful to God and humanity. And you know what? It is only then that our lives can produce sweetness. Don't be afraid to pass through the 'hot water' of life.

Don't be afraid to go through what God is willing to take you through. They can bend you, but surely, they will not break you! They are not to make you bitter, but better. The pain is for your gain!

Chapter 1: YOUR THOUGHT

"He (God) has made us accepted (to grace, endowed with special honour, be highly favoured) in the beloved"

(Ephesians 1:6).

Jacob looked at Joseph and saw a good son!

The ten brothers looked at Joseph and saw a useless dreamer!

The travellers looked at Joseph and saw a slave!!

Potiphar looked at Joseph and saw a fine servant!!

Potiphar's wife looked at Joseph and saw a potential boyfriend!

The prison officers saw in Joseph a prisoner!

How wrong they all were!

God looked at Joseph and saw a Prime Minister of Egypt in waiting!!

Don't be discouraged by what people see in you!!

Be encouraged by what God sees in you!!

Never underrate the person next to you

because you never know what the Lord has deposited in that person.

Your maid may be a Chief Executive Officer-in-waiting

for a company which shall employ your child.

Your garden-boy may be a president-in-waiting.

(Remember David got the anointing of becoming a King

while he was a simple child, herding sheep.

Esther was a simple orphan girl, yet she was a Queen-in-waiting).

Human perception can be viewed in three different dimensions. These three areas are very key to how far you go or not go in life (be it family, ministry or what have you). These dimensions are how you see yourself, how others see you and how God sees you.

These levels of perceptions would greatly determine your effectiveness, but are equally lethal when not handled well or harnessed properly. I must, however, quickly add here that your effectiveness as a Christian depends very much on whose perception you uphold.

How do you see yourself? Do you see yourself as a failure or success? Or as one who is inferior or equal to others? Are you a gossip or a confidant? A critic or an encourager? Difficult or easy to get along with? Domineering or submissive? Grumpy or gracious? Insecure or safe? Moody or motivated? Proud or humble? Given to hospitality or hostility? The list could go on.

If you honestly find yourself identifying with some of the negative aspects of these questions, then I encourage you to find good and trusted friends to whom you can open up for help. They should be people who can help address those areas, so as to appropriate right character traits and nurture them to becoming part of your being. Generally, negatives are 'life-drainers'; they sap our energy and take away the inspiration and motivation for living life, fully!

Sometimes, we find ourselves being unable to do certain things because we lack faith in ourselves; sometimes, it is the fear of making mistakes or the fear of mockery especially from people that know us. As a matter of fact, the greatest fear that some people dread is being alone, but you must understand that if you want to become outstanding in life, you have to first stand out and identify with what you want to become even if you will face reproach. It is in the process of enduring reproach that the glory takes over and you become outstanding. You have to believe strongly in the abilities that God has put in you.

Believing in yourself is a question of what you choose to believe about yourself. Stop doubting yourself, God has invested enough treasures in you to make you what He wants you to be. You have what it takes to create a new beginning in any circumstance that you find yourself, but when you doubt yourself, you despise the potential in you. What you need in order to live well is inside you; all you need to do is to discover it. You are to take a stand to disagree with people and circumstances that want to make you believe that you are a failure. You can prove them wrong, no matter how long you have failed.

It is our responsibility to work on ourselves and to develop a strong self-esteem, strive for excellence, do our absolute best every day, and love who we are, in and out. Where we do not love something about ourselves, then work toward s changing it. We are all on this journey of life to become better, do better, and live an extraordinary life. Let's begin to see ourselves for who we truly are: beautiful, strong and powerful.

When you believe the wrong things people say about you, your self-acceptance will be tampered with. If you use someone else as a standard for your life, you will be at the mercy of people. Difficulties in accepting who you are is also a contributory factor to losing self acceptance. When you are not content with who you are and not working to make it better, thus disliking some things about yourself, when equating family and friend's views of you to rejection, or you believe the society expects more from you than you can give, then your self-worth is at risk. Not forgetting too that when you look down on yourself and what you can do, or you become too proud to see or accept God's view of yourself, then you shortchanged yourself.

We must remember that we do not live just for our lives or simply to please or gain the approval of others, but it is very important to discover if we are saying or doing things that cause others "to take a wide berth" around us. Generally, people do not enjoy being in the company of negative characters. They make all kinds of excuses to avoid them.

With no intent for bigotry, or inciting anything, I'm going to make a reference, just to emphasize the extent of identity to a person, people, class, clan, race or what have you. When the Whites moved from Europe to Africa, they were described as 'Voyage of discovery'. When Africans moved from Africa to Europe, they were described as 'Illegal immigrants'. As a group of Africans in Europe, we are addressed as 'Refugees' while a group of Europeans in Africa are not forgotten to be addressed as 'Tourists'. When it is a group of Africans in the bush, it is classified as 'Poachers', while the Europeans in the bush are addressed as 'Hunters'. Black people working in foreign countries are 'foreigners' but the White people working in foreign countries are 'expatriates'.

The bottom line is, how do we see ourselves? If anything is going to change, it is how we see ourselves. If we let their view of us get into us, it will rule what we think and do. This is not good for us.

The best perception will ever be the way God sees you. You need to see yourself as God sees you because "as a man thinks in his heart, so he is" (Proverbs 23:7).

"Then the word of the LORD came unto me, saying,

Before I formed thee in the belly I knew thee; and before thou camest forth out of the womb I sanctified thee, and I ordained thee a prophet unto the nations.

Then said I, Ah, Lord GOD! behold, I cannot speak: for I am a child.

But the LORD said unto me, Say not, I am a child: for thou shalt go to all that I shall send thee, and whatsoever I command thee thou shalt speak”. (Jeremiah 1:4-7)

God sees you as being very special to Him. He believes in you! He has invested Himself in you through His finished work at Calvary. He has made you to be you; a very unique person with qualities and possibilities that only you can fulfill. Be encouraged to accept yourself as He accepts you and rise to be the person He has called you to be!

You are a child of God, held in honour and esteem by the Lord Who has redeemed you for Himself. His desire is to work in your life and character so that you can experience and fulfill the true purpose for which you were created. You were created by God Himself! And He never made anything bad, useless or unworthy. None of us had any say in being born, what sex we are, what our looks are with regard to the size of our ears, noses, etc. We need to accept the fact that God created us beautiful and full of potential to be very successful in life to the glory of His name.

Your greatest enemy is you and your greatest friend is you, because of what you believe or uphold of yourself. If you abandon yourself, then you will be abandoned, but you must understand that you are a person of great value. The reason why Satan is oppressing or opposing you is because you matter so much to God, the society and your generation. Don't let him stop you! It is true that the Bible warns against over-estimation of self (Luke 9:14), it does not say we should under-estimate ourselves either. You need to have the correct perception of yourself to make it in life. You must know who you are in Christ Jesus and the things that you can do by reason of the grace of God upon your life, so that nothing would distract you on your journey.

The whole message of the Scriptures is that we are "conquerors, overcomers, positive life-givers" in a sick and dying world. We are part of the answer, not part of the problem! The development of our character in the Christian service is, therefore, vital if our testimony is going to have an impact -- and you were created by God to make impact!

Chapter 2: YOUR SIGNIFICANT WORTH

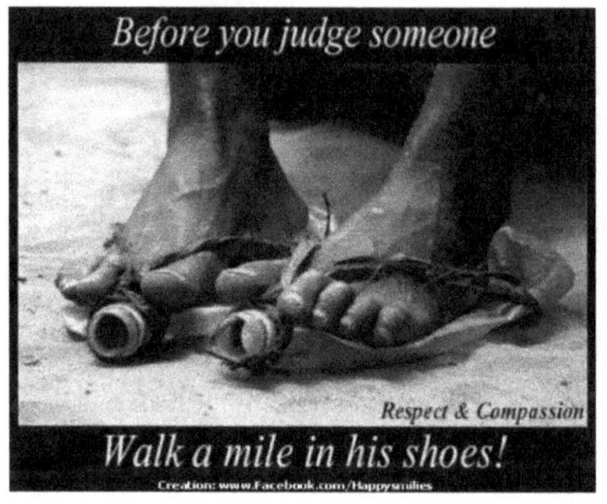

The world is so dynamic that things keep evolving faster than many people can keep pace with. What was generally the norm a few years ago has become obsolete today. New things are being created almost everyday. There are increasingly new approaches to life, business and ministry, to the extent that those who cannot keep pace have either become frustrated or have lost relevance.

One major challenge we face today is how to remain relevant in our communities. One way to maintain relevance wherever you find yourself is to stay within your God-ordained purpose. Your purpose is what determines your place of relevance. Jesus maintained His relevance while here on earth by sticking to the purpose of God for Him. Every product that no longer meets its purpose becomes irrelevant. Do you want to remain relevant? Stay within your God-ordained purpose. Find that one thing that God wants you to do and give your whole life to it.

Another secret of relevance is self-development. To maintain relevance, develop yourself. Self-development is essential to self-preservation. If you are working in an organisation and all you have is the Ordinary Level certificate, you are more likely to lose relevance. To maintain relevance in that organisation, you must study further to obtain additional qualifications relevant to your job description.

You must also learn to live for posterity and not prosperity to remain relevant. If you pursue prosperity to the detriment of posterity, you will soon lose relevance. God expects you to be a blessing and to leave a legacy behind. Maintaining relevance will equally require you to be knowledgeable. Knowledge is the key to living

(Hosea 4:6). You will never be known for what you don't know. For your light to shine, you must deal with ignorance at every level. In addition to that, you must learn to be creative and put your priorities in perspective. People easily fall for new things. We must allow God to do new things through us on a consistent basis.

The fame you want and the popularity you desire are already in you. All you need is to develop what you already have which is in you. Release it for the world to see and everybody will be clamouring to know you. The truth is, each one of us is uniquely gifted, for God did not create two people the same, neither for the same purpose. The difference in you is the potential, which, if discovered and developed, will make you a name.

Your next door is not your problem; your challenge at work is not your antagonist, not even your co-sellers in the market. Many are superstitious; always blaming their misfortunes on people or forces. Our belief in witches and wizards seems to be stronger than our belief in the Almighty God. I do not deny the existence of bad people or evil forces, but if you know what you carry and develop it, with God on your side, they will become your stepping-stones to higher heights.

Discovery is central to one's emancipation. The greatest plague in our society is lack of self-identity. Our tradition, culture, wrong values, and background have combined to kill the original person in us. Develop the gifts in you that differentiate you from all others. After discovery, develop them and release your gifts and potential to bless your generation.

Set your priorities right and follow them. Your first priority should be your personal relationship with God. Next should be your family. You should also know why you are in that career and pursue it with zeal.

Finally, live a pure life. God intends that every life be significant. You are salt and light. Salt loses its saltiness when it becomes impure, and light that is obstructed cannot shine for men to see. Purity is, therefore, an incontrovertible demand for those who desire to remain relevant.

THE GIANT SHIP ENGINE ENGINEER

A giant ship engine failed. The owners of the ship tried one expert after another, but none of them could figure out how to fix the engine. Then, they brought in an old man who had been fixing ships since he was a youngster. He carried a large bag of tools with him, and when he arrived, he immediately went to work. He inspected the engine very carefully, top to bottom.

Two of the ship's owners were there, watching this man, hoping he would know what to do. After looking things over, the old man reached into his bag and pulled out a small hammer. He gently tapped something. Instantly, the engine lurched into life. He carefully put his hammer away. The engine was fixed! A week later, the owners received a bill from the old man for ten thousand dollars.

"What!" exclaimed the owners; "he hardly did anything!"

So, they wrote the old man a note saying, "Please, send us an itemized bill."

The man sent a bill that read:

Tapping with a hammer .... $ 2.00

Knowing where to tap .... $ 9,998.00

Grand Total $10,000.00

Effort is important, but knowing where to make an effort in your life makes all the difference. I pray God to always give us the insight to know where to tap whenever we are faced with the dangers and worrisome situations associated with the decisions of today. May the good lord always bless our effort when we know where to tap (through His grace).

THE 500 NAIRA NOTE

Here is another story that may be familiar. I decided to use it because of the relevant lessons to the subject discussed in this chapter.

"It happened some time ago. I was in an audience listening to a motivational speaker.

The speaker brought out his wallet and pulled out a 500 Naira note. Holding it up, he asked: "Who wants this 500 naira note?" Lots of hands went up, including mine. A slow chorus began to build as people began to shout "Me!" "Me!" I began to wonder who the lucky one would be that the speaker would choose. And I also secretly wondered (and I am sure others did too) why he would simply give away 500 naira. Even as the shouts of "I want it" grew louder, I noticed a young woman running down the aisle. She ran up onto the stage, went up to the speaker, and grabbed the five 500 naira note from his hand. "Well done, young lady," said the speaker into the microphone.

The speaker simply said "Most of us just sit and wait for good things to happen. That's of no use. You've got to make things happen. Make a move. Simply thinking about doing something is of no use and not good enough."

Our lives are like that. We all see opportunities around us; we all want the good things, but the problem is that we don't take action. We all wanted the 500 naira note on offer, but we didn't make the move. We looked at it longingly. Get up and do something about it. Don't worry about what other people might think.

Take action!

Later, the speaker got another 500 naira note and held it up for all to see. I thought I knew what's up, but he just asked a simple question: "How much is this worth?" "Five Hundred naira!" the crowd yelled in unison. "Right," said the speaker. He then took the note and crumpled it into a ball and asked, "How much is it worth now?"

"Five Hundred naira!" screamed the audience. He then threw the note on the ground, stamped all over it and picked it up and asked one more time: "And how much is it worth now?" "Five Hundred naira!" was the response. "I want you to remember this," said the speaker. "Just because someone crumples it, or stamps on it, the value of the note does not diminish. We should all be like the 500 naira note!

In our lives, there might be times when we feel crushed, stamped over and beaten. But never let your self-worth diminish. Just because someone chooses to crush you, doesn't change your worth one bit! Don't allow your self-worth to diminish because someone says something nasty or does something dirty to you."

Never let your self worth diminish.

I AM AN EAGLE, NOT A CHICKEN

The story was told of a hunter who killed an eagle and brought the eagle's egg for his hen (female chicken) to hatch along with her eggs. Later, the eaglet reef among the chicken; the hen became the mother of the eaglet. But one day, the eaglets saw another eagle fly high above the storm. So, he asks the mother hen, what kind of bird is that? She replied, that was an eagle, you are a hen (chicken), you cannot fly like that. Three out of four eaglets lived and died as a chicken, except one.

As he grew older, their mother followed them no more to the garbage looking for food, believing they are mature. As they saw an eagle coming to their direction, they all ran under a tree where there was a broken glass and this eaglet looked at its face in the mirror and got frightened, believing it was an eagle, because they are the same. It also discovered that it could understand eagle's language better than chickens as the eagle was saying, "Today, I will eat this and reserve some for tomorrow."

He now realized that it was not a chicken, and it replied 'I am not a chicken, but an eagle and eagle can't eat eagle', but the eagle replied,

'If you are truly an eagle, what are you doing down there, for eagles don't scavenge but fly, why running from battles like a chick from eagles' attack. Why eating and talking like chicken."

This word motivated him to fly for the first time and soar higher. Many were born eagle, raised from adopted parents, lived and behaved like fowls and died as chickens.

THE MEANINGLESS COMPARISONS

A crow lived in the forest and was absolutely satisfied in life. But one day, he saw a swan. "This swan is so white and I am so black," the crow thought. "This swan must be the happiest bird in the world."

He expressed his thoughts to the swan. "Actually," the swan replied, "I was feeling that I was the happiest bird around until I saw a parrot which has two colours. I now think the parrot is the happiest bird in creation."

The crow then approached the parrot and the parrot explained: "I lived a very happy life—until I saw a peacock. I have only two colours, but the peacock has multiple colours."

The crow then visited a peacock in the zoo and saw that hundreds of people had gathered to see him. After the people had left, the crow approached the peacock:

Dear peacock, you are so beautiful; everyday thousands of people come to see you. "When people see me, they immediately shove me away."

"I think you are the happiest bird on the planet," said the crow.

The peacock replied, "I always thought that I was the most beautiful and happy bird on the planet. But because of my beauty, I am entrapped in this zoo. I have examined the zoo very carefully, and I have realized that the crow is the only bird not kept in a cage. So for the past few days, I have been thinking that if I were a crow, I could happily roam everywhere."

That's our problem too. We make unnecessary comparison with others and become sad. We don't value what God has given us. This all leads to the vicious cycle of unhappiness. Value who God has made you to be and the things God has given you.

Learn the secret of being happy and discard the comparisons, which lead only to unhappiness.

Chapter 3: YOUR PURPOSE, VISION AND SERVICE

In 2 Chronicles 26, we read of a very successful king by the name Uzziah. He came to power at a young age (16) and allowed a spiritual man (Zechariah) to impart into his life. Zechariah was a man who lived under an open heaven, because "he had understanding in the visions of God" (v. 5). That word "understanding" is a spiritual word meaning "to separate, distinguish, to discern, to mark, to understand, all which depend on the power of separating, distinguishing, specially to discern, perceive" (Wilson's). The word "vision" here is "to see in vision, i. e. to be taught of God in vision as the prophets" (Wilson's). Zechariah received spiritual revelation from God and passed it on to Uzziah.

Zechariah and Uzziah were a great combination. As a result, Uzziah was "always ahead of" the other kings and nations around him. It was not until he allowed pride to enter his heart that things went horribly wrong for him. He stepped outside his realm of authority and offered incense in the temple, which was not his job to do. He ignored the warnings and the judgment of God fell. Uzziah came out of the temple a leper, and remained a leper until he died. Pride closed the heaven over Uzziah, then the nation of Israel.

Spiritually, things went into decline. The revelation of God could no longer be obeyed.

It wasn't until Uzziah died that we saw the heaven opened again over Israel. We read about that in Isaiah 6. "In the year that King Uzziah died, I saw also the Lord sitting upon a throne . . ." The voice, revelation, vision of God came again through Prophet Isaiah. He brought a new season of the voice and revelation of God, calling the people to commit themselves to the service of God: "Whom shall I send? And who will go for us?"

If you don’t know what you are looking for, when you see it, you will not recognize it! Do you have the plan of God for your life? And why you are in that place, you don't need any herbalist to tell you that. Do you have a vision of God for your life!

Strategic vision possesses real power in setting direction, motivating action, and guiding decisions. The following can not be overemphasized when it comes to Vision:

Visions must be coherent; integrating goals, strategies, and action plans into a complete and recognizable picture of the future organization and its environment.

Visions must be powerful to be able to generate commitment and motivate performance.

A vision emphasizes what an individual or an organization can be.

Visions should be realistic about what the future may hold, and about what is achievable within the chosen time frame.

Visions build on these statements to describe the future size, shape, and texture of the organization.

Visions express the goals of an organization at a particular time. The true mature fellow uses all three to guide and empower the organization toward its goals.

Visions must be detailed.

Just because a man of vision is ruling the world, there are men of faith and ideas.

They mind what God says not what people say; they are men who despise tradition than what God says. God is waiting for you and this will be the beginning of your greatness. Pursuit of vision is pursuing God's master plan for your life. Show me a man of vision and I will show you a man of glorious destiny.

The visionless will end up serving those who have vision. Methuselah who lived for 969 years without a significant record of what he achieved in those years was just marking time. Joseph at the age of 17 already knew where he was going. He had a dream, he had a vision, he was focused and he started working towards his dreams, even at a tender age, but his elder brothers had no dreams, no vision and no direction.

No wonder, Joseph’s brothers eventually became his subjects! We have many teenagers who are just living their lives purposelessly. Let's not even talk about many adults who are just jumping from pillar to post without a purpose. Moses discovered his purpose at the age of 80, yet he left a landmark in his generation. So maybe, age is not really a barrier. If you don't have a plan for your life, people will plan how you are going to live your life for you. the best vision, however, is the god-given vision because such a vision will always receive heaven’s backing.

Do you have any vision yet? If no, talk to God and He will reveal His plans and purpose for your life. There is a treasure in you!

Every product is manufactured to serve a specific purpose! Hence, you should find out the reason for your existence and know what to do! A discovery of purpose is essentially for possession and the disposition to serve the need of others. Service is the only way to actualise your purpose and fulfil your destiny. If you are on earth to consume only, you will end up dispossessed! True greatness is the discovery of what you are created for and actualising that purpose. No matter how anointed, gifted or enlightened you are, if you lack purpose, you will not become accomplished; that's the gospel truth!

Your degree of commitment to service determines your ultimate level in the race of life. No matter your purpose, it must be rooted in service. You are running with a vision, going on a mission or burning with a passion. If you are not in any of these three, then life is a burden". Living for self makes a servant, but living for others makes a leader.

Chapter 4: DISCOVERING YOUR TREASURE

Martin Luther King Jnr. said "If any man has no purpose for living, he is not fit to live" and 'Men of purpose are known to be men of impact". You are not formed by your father and mother. They were only channels through which the formation took place. So, you did not just happen; you were consciously created. You are a child of destiny, so you cannot afford to live like a destitute. In the journey of discovery, you will need the input of the following:

MENTORSHIP

A mentor is a person or friend who guides a less experienced person by building trust and modeling positive behaviors. An effective mentor understands that his or her role is to be dependable, engaged, authentic, and tuned into the needs of the mentee (i.e. the one that is being mentored).

To stand out, you need a mentor, not a tormentor. Mentors maintain and remold destinies. Peter told the crippled man at the Beautiful Gate in Acts chapter 3, "Look on us!" (In other words, he seemed to be saying, 'If I am crippled, you can remain crippled. If I am on the ground, you can be on the ground. If I am begging, you can beg. If people have to carry me, then they have to carry you.') "Such as I have, I give unto you. In the name of Jesus, rise up and walk". It is impossible for a man to give what he doesn't have, no matter how interested he is.

You must be careful under whose ministry you surrender your life, because no matter how hard you try, you cannot outgrow the testimony of your mentor. If God has positioned somebody in your life as a mentor over you, you will reject what is not his testimony in your own life; you will reject what is not in his identity. You will reject it! I cannot be the son of a lion and be eating rotten flesh; I can't be the son of an eagle and be messing up like a vulture. You will reject it! If you can't find it in him, you reject it in your own life. You also take a look at them anytime you are feeling depressed. Anytime it looks like things are not working, open back to what God has said to you. You also take a look at these things anytime you are confronted in a battle.

When David faced Goliath, he recalled how God had delivered him from the bear and the lion. Paul was a great mentor to Timothy. He instructed him, he gave him leadership role and even guided him on how to go about it. He made himself available for any questions from Timothy. To him, he was a father when father was away.

To unveil the treasure in you, you need the input of mentors. These are not just role models. They, in their capacity are there to show the way, walk the way and encourage to go in the way. More than often, their roles are so personal and intimate, even if they may not be physically available, sometimes because of necessity's sake.

DISCIPLINE

Discipline is the bridge between goals and accomplishment. The best time to set up a new discipline is when the idea is strong. One discipline always leads to another discipline. All disciplines affect each other.

Discipline is the foundation upon which all success is built. Lack of it inevitably leads to failure. In the words of Jim John, "Discipline has within it the potential for creating future miracles."

The most effective way to prevent what is bad is to promote what is good. The best way to influence behaviour is not to control and regulate, but to inspire and motivate.

You get more for your efforts when they are applied in a positive direction. Instead of fighting against what you dislike, work to build and support what you value and desire.

The answer to despair is not to despise it, for that only adds to it. The answer is to overwhelm it with goodness and love. Focus your attention and energy on what works, and make more of it. Celebrate what is good and right, useful and valuable; and allow it to grow.

Nurture, promote and support what you love about life. Delight in good things, and give the power of your joy to them. Be a positive force by acting with positive purposes. Give your awareness and energy to the good side of life, and make it stronger than ever.

CO-ORDINATION

"For which of you desiring to build a tower, does not first sit down and count the cost, whether he has enough to complete it?" (Luke 14:28)

Coordination is a part of discipline, but it will be discussed separately, here. If you fail to plan, you have planned to fail. Many people are not organized, that is why their things don't galvanize. Be organized in your looks and in all you do. When you are well organized, you gain speed and maximum results. There are no disorganized successful people and there are also no organized defeated people. In all you do, take time to train and to plan. There are many who still have the assumption that things will sort themselves out. That is an assumption in futility. Spend time to organize your things, so as not to waste time rearranging things.

Setting priority is also a product of proper co-ordination. All you desire to do cannot be done at the same time. Even, resources are always limited, therefore, setting priority is inevitable if you are a good planner, though. Establish your goals for without the goal posts, there will never be a winner in any soccer game. In the same manner, until you set goals, you cannot win goals. What are the things you want in life? Set them out clearly.

Be organized; be disciplined, outline your things in order of preference. Before you step out each morning, draw your programme of activities and attach time to them. Keep a workable diary; you will be better with it. Make sure you stick to your plans. Many things will fight against your arrangement; do not give in if you want to fulfill your purpose.

maximum results. There are no disorganized [illegible] organized dedicated schedule. Until you do that, it's time to make [illegible] why [illegible] the [illegible] challenging times.

Getting priority is [illegible]

Without the goal [illegible]

[illegible] discipline, they [illegible] procrastinate [illegible] activities [illegible] plans. Make [illegible] arrangements [illegible] you want to fulfill your purpose.

LIVING BEYOND THE SURFACE

God's plan for you is to live beyond the surface. The average man lives behind a mask. His smiles, his laughter, his piety, his show of confidence are all parts of the role he is playing. Seldom, if ever, does he let anyone know what he really is. Only in times of pain, fear or perhaps, when he has had too much to drink does his mask down and we see him as he really is.

There was a time when a storey building rooms of officers were to be built in the city of Lagos for a church. Before the construction work started, the builder wanted to test the soil around the base of the existing foundation to make sure it could take the additional weight. He did not want to run the risk of having the house tilt or the floor crack as the earth settled.

One day, a team of geological engineers came to the site. They had a clever kind of drill that punched a small hole in the earth, going about twenty feet and coming back up with samples of the various layers of soil. They discovered that the surface sand was only about three feet deep. After that, it changed to a sandy type of clay, then another type of sand, and finally bedrock. They concluded the soil could easily stand the additional weight of the second storey.

Later on, I went to the spot and stood, looking at the sand sample they had dumped on the grass. Suddenly, I started wondering what would happen if someone should take a similar boring of my life. After the surface over my life, how far can the boring go before discovery is made that inside areas in the deep is full of me? Know despairingly that they would find Jesus Christ in great abundance on the surface in many lives. But we need to go beyond the surface, in the deep areas of our lives, in the subconscious.

Yet, my desire was that such a drilling would reveal Jesus Christ all the way down to the bottom of my life. I wanted to be so pure that when I was cut, I would bleed Jesus. I thought of that story in the seventh chapter of Acts where Stephen was stoned.

The Bible says that the surface of two different lives were broken that afternoon. Stephen's words to the religious leaders cut down to their hearts going beyond the surface. What was revealed? Hatred, bitterness and murder! They reacted so violently that they dragged Stephen through the streets of the city and stoned him to death. But as Stephen was cut with the stone, also going beyond the surface of his life, instead of reacting, he responded with such positive love that eventually one of those involved in the stoning, a Pharisee named Saul, was converted.

That afternoon, I was convinced by this revelation that I wanted to be like that. But how could it be? My life, it seemed, was learning to handle the junk that was falling into it on daily basis. What could I do about the dregs which had long since settled below the surface and rose only in times of stress, anger, or temptation?

The answer came, "walk in the spirit, and you shall not fulfill the lust of the flesh" (Gal.5:16), similar promise was made in Ephesians 3:16, 17. And again he said, "Put off concerning the former conversation of the old man which is corrupt according to deceitful lust and be renewed in the spirit of your mind" (Eph.4:2,23).

So, what I desired was not an impossible. In fact, it was to be the goal of every follower of Jesus Christ. A Christian must daily stand guard at the doorpost of his mind to repel each evil thought by which Satan would gain entry. Let us be committed to a walk of absolute obedience to Christ in our conscious life. It is possible.

Chapter 5: HONING YOUR CRAFT

Friend, is there any talent that God has put into your hands? Is there any uncommon ability that you have? Is there something that you do better than everyone around you? Is there any skill you possess that distinguishes you from your peers? Is there any ability that you either have naturally or acquired by learning?

God says trade with your talents. Use your skills and make gains with your areas of strength. Sharpen and improve your skills, brand your talents and take them to the marketplace, and you will be shocked at the gains you will make.

"The soul of the sluggard desireth, and hath nothing: but the soul of the diligent shall be made fat" (Proverbs 13:4).

Nobody has any business being poor in life, judging by the incredible potential and talents the creator has put in everyone. Please know that you are too loaded to fail; you are too talented to remain small.

Know that no one will pay for your talents in their raw form. As precious as gold is, if you see it in its raw form, it will not make any serious meaning to you; same for crude oil. They are only useful and valuable when refined. In the same way, when you refine what you have, then and only then does it command a high value! Many are forever wishing they have what others have. I always tell them, they miss the real point. The truth is that no one needs whatever he or she does not have to make it in life. What you have is good enough if you will discover them and take them to the refinery.

Discover what you have for it is the first responsibility which God has given you. The word of God says it is the glory of God to hide a thing, but it is the joy of the king to discover it. Know that so many things are lying dormant in you, waiting to be discovered. Turn inward to unearth the treasures resident inside of you. There is no such thing as ungifted or untalented. Please discover what you have.

Development is vital. This is the refining stage, where raw materials are worked on. The question is: how do you develop or refine your potential? By studying, training and practicing. In II Timothy 2:15, the Bible says, "study to show yourself approved". In the areas where you notice your gift, enroll for studies and do serious training to harvest your full potential.

Display your talent for sale. There are many willing buyers of your refined products. In its raw form, no one wants it, but when refined and displayed, they will come for it at your price. This is the expressway to your greatness. It is your time; arise and shine!

Newton's third law of motion states:

"A body at rest will continue to remain at rest unless an external force is applied on it".

Action sets a journey of success in motion. As you know, there is promotion when you are in motion. The Almighty God chose to put his great ideas into use which is why we have a place like the earth to dwell on today. In Genesis 1:3, "And God said, let there be light and there was light". Putting what you have into use will help such to multiply. No matter how divine a gift or talent is, without usage or doing something with it, it will not increase.

Abundance is found where increase already is. In Matt. 25:29 "For unto everyone that hath shall be given, and he shall have abundance". It is doing or putting what you have into use that creates room for increase. Without work, no increase would be possible, for in all labour, there is profit. Moses had a wonderful weapon in his hand, but was frightened by the Egyptian magicians. He realized how great the rod in his hand was, after dropping it on the ground according to God's instruction. What you hold on to can hardly multiply. A beautiful building that is not inhabited will soon be ruined.

"And the Lord said unto him, what is that in thine hand? And he said a rod".

Many people think the things which they need to start what they want to do in life is what they do not have. Rest assured that what you have is good enough to start what you want to do. God, the creator of heaven and earth, started the creation project with nothing; no material substance, except that He spoke; He started with words. The Bible says, "the power of death and life are in the mouth".

In fact, your own case is better because you have some things. It may not be up to what you expect and it does not have to be. No one who made it in life ever had all he or she wanted before embarking on the voyage of destiny. Moses at the bank of the Red Sea, just as he led the Israelites out of Egypt, felt helpless, but God called his attention to the rod in his hand. With it, the Red Sea that initially looked intimidating was divided.

In the wilderness, with just five loaves of bread and two small fishes, Jesus fed over 5,000 people. So, stop looking for more; what you have is good enough, start with it - the little money from your savings, the skill, the people you know, your enormous strength as a young person, the goodwill, the idea, the time, the space, the talent and many other things.

Discover what you have: look inward, look around, take a stock of your potential and abilities, and gather your resources together; and something beautiful will come out of them. What you have is enough if you can plan. A good planner will use little to achieve much. You cannot get it done until you get started. Start now for procrastination is a crippler of destiny.

FOR QUALITY AND EXCELLENCE

"And the king speak unto Ashpenaz the master of his eunuchs, that he should bring certain of the children of Israel, and of the king's seed, and of the princes; Children in whom was no blemish, but well favoured, and skilful in all wisdom, and cunning in knowledge, and understanding science, and such as had ability in them to stand in the king's palace, and whom they might teach the learning and the tongue of the Chaldeans (Daniel 1:3-4).

Quality is essential. I implore you to be a man or woman of value. When you insist on quality, you become qualified for excellence. Besides, only quality things last. If you are a person of "anything goes", to go forward will be difficult. So, in all you do or buy, insist on quality.

If you love cheap things, you will discover that you spend more money all the time because you have to buy the same thing all over again. A poor quality article is costlier than a high quality one because you will have to buy repeatedly.

Being a woman or man of quality is a mentality which you should develop and maintain. If you produce goods, insist on and maintain quality; but also increase the quantity produced. Quantity does not necessarily decrease quality if you have built up your capacity to accommodate the increase.

Set a standard for your thing. In every nation, there is standard organization which is a body set up to ensure that products are standardized and of good quality. No nation wants to become a dumping ground for inferior goods. Likewise, do not be a trash bin, set a minimum standard for your life and things.

Quality control is essential. There is no way you can ensure quality, except you put control measures in place. Have a policy, do not just go for anything or imbibe everything. While controlling, think of increase or enlargement. Have a goal for more and do not remain where you have always been. Life is dynamic. If you do not move with it; you will soon be left behind. Every shame in your life is turned to fame in Jesus' name.

"Seest thou a man diligent in his business? He shall stand before kings; he shall not stand before mean men" (Proverbs 22:29). No matter what you are doing or the task that lies ahead, the best way to develop yourself is through training. Whatever your chosen field, learn how to do it well because interest may create the zeal, only training will ensure the skill. Know that we are in a competitive world, and for any to fare well, he or she must be ready for competition. Competitiveness, therefore, is only feasible when you are current. If you are not, you will not be able to flow with current changes.

The question is: In what area are you deficient? Find out and fill the gap by undergoing training in that field. In 2Timothy 1:16, the Bible says "wherefore I put thee in remembrance that thou stir up the gift of God which is in thee by the putting on of my hands". So, wherever you notice a gift, stir it up.

Identify your field: Know what you are created for and work towards becoming an authority in it. Know that you cannot become a champion in all fields – but the particular one you are cut out for should not be wasted.

Broaden your horizon. Do not limit yourself to what you already know; expand your coast through training. Are you a student, minister of God, vocation expert or a civil servant, etc? Develop yourself in the area of your calling. Get relevant knowledge to stand out.

Do not rest on your current level of attainment; carry out researches. Be current and stop operating with obsolete methods for there are modern ways of doing things. Repackage and change certain things about yourself. Remember, if you are not updated, you may be downgraded.

Prepare for opportunities. Acquire new skills, for no knowledge is a waste. Whatever chance comes your way, use it for something worthwhile. Learn how to drive vehicles, enroll for computer training if you have not done so. This is because you cannot be a global personality if you are not computer literate.

Chapter 6: WHAT OBSTACLES? WHAT EXCUSES?

Whatever course you may have chosen to pursue, there will always be obstacles. This must be made clear to you that victory is not the absence of battles; it is the ability to prevail in battles. The number of battles you fight in life depends on how high you wish to rise because greater prices are paid for bigger accomplishments.

Obstacles come in various forms and at different stages of life. Some in the form of human agents - a boss at work, a colleague together on an assignment, a next door neighbour, a co – seller in the market, a competitor in the industry, a distant relation etc. Some people may just think you have to be stopped. They may hate your result and your face or just find it difficult to stand your guts. Obstacles may also be spiritual in nature and origin. For no just cause, you may sometimes find yourself in needless crisis or inexplicable struggles and you wonder why?

Failure to locate purpose is the foundation of all human sufferings and frustrations and a self-inflicted obstacle. If you are confused as to what really is your God-given assignment on earth, stop and find out before you make further efforts because the race of life is not won by trial and error. You have to be definite about your life's pursuit.

Having secured your dream, do not abandon or change it, no matter the pressure. This note of warning is important because your dream will be challenged, no matter who you are. Situations will develop around you that will tempt you to doubt, drop, amend, compromise or change what you originally set out to do. Circumstances and situations do change arbitrarily; except on a very strong conviction, do not change your original dream.

Joseph held on tenaciously to his dreams. Many temptations, frustrations and contradictions confronted him, but he refused to give up. Hold on to your dreams, no matter what, because your situation will not remain the same. Dreams have no expiry date; no matter how long, tough and rough, make sure you become what you originally dreamt to be.

MTN came to Nigeria at a time when nobody wanted to invest in Nigeria; at a time when Nigerians did not have phones. Even Zenith Bank refused to loan MTN cash to operate, UBA rejected MTN's offer, but today, see the difference! At least, we all know the story of the only unelected civilian President in Nigeria - Goodluck

Jonathan. We know how the people said he was not going to be President; they even made him acting President. Today, the rest is history.

What about Cowbell? When they came to Nigeria, they made milk in sachets. Peak laughed at them, they said Cowbell was milk for the poor. But they were right! 3 million poor people could afford N10 a day for a sachet of milk. Now, do the mathematics: 3 million people buying milk at N10.00 - that was N30million every single day. In a month, they grossed N900million (almost N1billion). Even Peak had to make sachet milk in order to survive in the market.

So, what have people told you? What have they said you cannot do, or you are not qualified for, or you do not have experience for? They told Cowbell, they told Goodluck, they told MTN, but today their stories have changed! I have a feeling something is changing for you today! They will change their strategies, just to keep pace with you. Don't listen to what people are saying or what life is showing you. YES, YOU CAN. Success is not about where you graduated from, or what grade you graduated with, but what graduates out of you.

The one thing successful people never do

Success comes in all shapes and colours. You can be successful in your job and career. You can equally be successful in your marriage, in sports or hobbies. Whatever success you are after, there is one thing all radically successful people have in common: Their ferocious drive and hunger for success makes them to never give up.

Successful people (or the people talking or writing about them) often paint a picture of the perfect ascent to success. In fact, some of the most successful people in business, entertainment and sport have failed. Many have failed numerous times, but they have never given up. Successful people are able to pick themselves up, dust themselves off and carry on trying.

I have collected some examples that should be an inspiration to anyone who aspires to be successful. They show that if you want to succeed, you should expect failure along the way. I actually believe that failure can spur you on and make you try even harder. You could argue that every experience of failure increases the hunger for success. The truly successful won't be beaten; they take responsibility for failure, learn from it and start all over from a stronger position.

Henry Ford - The pioneer of modern business entrepreneurship and founder of the Ford Motor Company failed a number of times on his route to success. His first venture to build a motor car got dissolved a year and half after it was started because the stockholders lost confidence in Henry Ford. Ford was able to gather enough capital to start again, but a year later, pressure from the financiers forced him out of the company again. Despite the fact that the entire motor industry had lost faith in him, he managed to find another investor to start the Ford Motor Company; and the rest is history.

Walt Disney - One of the greatest business leaders who created the global Disney Empire of film studios, theme parks and consumer products didn't start off successful. Before the great success, came a number of failures. Believe it or not, Walt was fired from an early job at the Kansas City Star Newspaper because he was not creative enough! In 1922, he started his first company called Laugh-O-Gram. The Kansas-based business would produce cartoons and short advertising films. In 1923, the business went bankrupt. Walt didn't give up, he packed up, went to Hollywood and started The Walt Disney Company.

Richard Branson - He is undoubtedly a successful entrepreneur with many successful ventures to his name including Virgin Atlantic, Virgin Music and

Virgin Active. However, when he was 16, he dropped out of school to start a student magazine that didn't do as well as he hoped. He then set up a mail-order record business which did so well that he opened his own record shop called Virgin. Along the way to success, came many other failed ventures including Virgin Cola, Virgin Vodka, Virgin Clothes, Virgin Vie, Virgin cards etc.

Oprah Winfrey - She ranks No 1 in the Forbes celebrity list and is recognized as the queen of entertainment, based on an amazing career as an iconic talk show host, media proprietor, actress and producer. In her earlier career, she had numerous setbacks which included getting fired from her job as a reporter because she was 'unfit for television', getting fired as co-anchor for the 6 O'clock weekday news on WJZ-TV and being demoted to morning TV.

J. K. Rowling - She wrote the Harry Potter books, selling over 400 million copies and making it one of the most successful and lucrative book and film series ever. However, like so many writers, she received endless rejections from publishers. Many rejected her manuscript outright for reasons like 'it was far too long for a children's book' or because 'children books never make any money'. J. K. Rowling's story is even more inspiring because when she started, she was a divorced single mum on welfare.

Bill Gates - Co-founder and chairman of Microsoft, set up a business called Traf-O-Data. The partnership between him, Paul Allen and Paul Gilbert was based on a good idea (to read data from roadway traffic counters and create automated reports on traffic flows), but a flawed business model that left the company with few customers. The company ran up losses between 1974 and 1980 before it was closed. However, Bill Gates and Paul Allen took what they learned and avoided those mistakes when they created the Microsoft Empire.

Jan Koum Brian, the Founder of WhatsApp. A former employee of Yahoo, having lost his both parents, he used to sweep the floor of a cheap grocery store just to survive. A part of that money was used to feed himself and then the other to buy second-hand programming and networking books. In 2009, feeling competent enough, he applied for a job with Twitter, but was turned down! In 2010, he applied for another job with Facebook where he was offered a mere appointment, but 4 years later, one of his personal projects is today the chat messenger called WhatsApp. And this year, it was acquired for a whopping 19 Billion Dollars by the same Facebook that gave him a mere appointment when he was turned down. It is the biggest IT deals in recent times!

History is littered with many more similar examples. Milton Hershey failed in his first two attempts to set up a confectionery business. H. J. Heinz set up a company that produced horseradish, which went bankrupt shortly after. Steve Jobs got fired from Apple, the company he founded, only to return a few years later to turn it into one of the most successful companies ever.

"The soul of the sluggard craves, and gets nothing, while the soul of the diligent is richly supplied" (Proverbs 13:4)

Not giving up until the desired success is achieved is what separates boys from men. This is so because nothing in life is easy; whoever will get to the top must be ready to climb up. Though, climbing is not an easy task, but it does not mean it is impossible. Mount Everest is reputed to be the highest mountain in the world, yet men have climbed it. Also, River Mississippi is the longest river; men traced it to its source. That shows that no assignment is too tough for the one who is ready and determined to succeed. Keep making attempts; do not ever consider giving up on your task, no matter how difficult, and no matter how many times you have tried with no results.

Life is not kind to anyone, you have to give it a fight by facing your assignment squarely and refusing to accept defeat, deciding not to give up on what you believe must be done. Life is like a giant holding on to your things and saying "I know they belong to you, but if you can dare me, come for them".

No matter how beaten and battered a wrestler is in the ring, if he is still on his feet, the fight continues.

That is how life is; you may be down, but please do not be out. You might have been pursuing a thing for many years till now; I implore you not to lose hope because God is set to perfect your situation this year. You must also know that everyone up there today was once down. Everybody gets knocked down at one time or the other. No matter how careful one may be, certain things will still go wrong. It is a measure of grace to develop some shock absorbers.

There are many areas of life where people get knocked down - marriage, business and relationships. There are mistakes and miscalculations that some of us do make too, but whatever the case is, if you get knocked down, refuse to be knocked out.

Chapter 7: GOLDEN THOUGHTS

These are well thought out food for the soul. In ruminating on them, I believe you will find courage to give expression the treasure you are and the treasure in you.

"Worrying does not empty tomorrow of its troubles, it empties today of its strength."

Lesson: Identify what has been holding you back from your career success. Most likely, it's been worry and fear. It's time to leave fear behind. The things you are afraid of are often the things most worth doing.

"The best way to predict the future is to invent it." – Alan Kay

Lesson: You can't wait around for good things to happen this year; you need to make them happen yourself.

"Strive not to be a success, but rather to be of value." – Albert Einstein

Lesson: Bringing value to your company is the best way up the corporate ladder. Don't play office politics, just make sure you bring as much value as you possibly can to your organization.

"Every strike brings me closer to the next home run." – Babe Ruth

Lesson: You can learn and grow from your mistakes if you see them not as mere errors, but as opportunities to grow as a professional and as a person.

"If I had six hours to chop down a tree, I'd spend the first four hours sharpening the axe." – Abraham Lincoln

Lesson: Before you start a job hunt or a new project, make sure you've sharpened your skills, so you can succeed.

"Courage is being scared to death, but saddling up anyway." – John Wayne

Lesson: You should try to frequently do things which scare you and push you outside your comfort zone. Take on a complicated new project, offer to do some public speaking, or learn a new skill. You'll never rise in your career if you don't take the chance to fall.

"A business that makes nothing, but money is a poor business." – Henry Ford

Lesson: Sure the bottom line is important, but it's not the only thing. A business should be more than money signs; it should give something back to the world and inspire passion in employees.

"Success is walking from failure to failure with no loss of enthusiasm." – Winston Churchill

Lesson: In the new year, it's important not to let the little things get you down. You won't hit a home run every time, but if you bounce back you'll come back stronger.

"It always seems impossible until it's done." – Nelson Mandela

Lesson: Nothing is ever impossible, even if it often feels that way. If you give up too soon, you'll never know if you could have actually achieved your dream.

"Successful and unsuccessful people do not vary greatly in their abilities. They vary in their desires to reach their potential." – John Maxwell

Lesson: Don't write yourself off before you actually try. If you put in hard work and effort this year, you'll be closer to achieving your dream.

"When one door of happiness closes, another opens, but often we look so long at the closed door that we do not see the one that has been opened for us." – Helen Keller

Lesson: There will always be negatives in your professional life. If you focus on the negative, instead of the positive, you'll miss out on great opportunities.

"Without ambition one starts nothing. Without work one finishes nothing. The prize will not be sent to you. You have to win it." – Ralph Waldo Emerson

Lesson: The best way to succeed is to marry pie-in-the-sky ambition with hard work. If you dream big and work hard, you'll be able to make those dreams a reality.

"There are no traffic jams along the extra mile." – Roger Staubach

Lesson: Going the extra mile is really the best way to arrive at your dream destination. No one ever made it to his or her dream career, got their dream job, or started a business without going above and beyond.

“Dreaming, after all, is a form of planning.” – Gloria Steinem

Lesson: It’s hard to get anywhere in your professional or personal life without a little bit of dreaming. You need a destination in mind to start right, so don’t be afraid to dream big.

The PAST is a WASTE PAPER; the PRESENT is a NEWSPAPER, the FUTURE is a QUESTION PAPER, so read and write carefully; otherwise, LIFE will be a TISSUE PAPER

A dream is not what you see while asleep. It is what does not let you sleep!

The most beautiful people we have known are those who have known defeat, suffering, struggle, lost and have found their way out of the depths.

No one ever becomes poor by giving and no one ever becomes rich by begging. Which group do you belong?

"Your thoughts are the architects of your destiny."

"One cannot think crooked and walk straight."

"The only limit to our realization of tomorrow will be our doubts of today. Let us move forward with strong and active faith."

"The great use of life is to spend it for something that will outlast it."

"When I stand before God at the end of my life, I would hope that I would not have a single bit of talent left, and could say, "I used everything you gave me".

"If you take responsibility for yourself, you will develop a hunger to accomplish your dreams."

"Only as high as I reach can I grow, Only as far as I seek can I go, Only as deep as I look can I see, Only as much as I dream can I be”

“All our dreams can come true, if we have the courage to pursue them.”

We make a living by what we get. We make a life by what we give {What do you give?}

Destiny is not a matter of chance, it is a matter of choice; it is a thing to be achieved.

Brethren, you can fast for ten thousand days and cry for a whole year, without a seed in the ground, there is NOTHING to harvest. You can speak in tongues for all you want, without a seed there is NOTHING to harvest. A farmer that eats all his seeds and does not sow some will have nothing to harvest in the future. Brethren, God responds to your seed, not your tears. He is a God of principles. You must sow good seeds.

Always remember that whatever you make happen for others, God will make happen for you.

What is it that thing, you will regret not doing when you grow old?

"A man's doubts and fears are his worst enemies."

"Failure should be our teacher, not our undertaker. Failure is delay not defeat. It is a temporary detour, not a dead end."

The quality of your mind is the total quality of your life. You may lose other battles, but don't lose the battle of your mind. If your mind is not delivered, every aspect of your life is not delivered.

Remember that decisions are too important to leave to chance, always reach for the best that is within you.

PRAYER POINTS

I pull down the stronghold of confusion in my life in the name of Jesus.

Every seat of confusion in my life, be broken down in the name of Jesus.

Let the storm and cloud of confusion within my mind be still in the name of Jesus.

I claim a sound mind in the name of Jesus.

Every faulty foundation in my life, receive the fire of God in the name of Jesus.

I fire back every arrow of mind destruction fired into my life back to sender in the name of Jesus.

My mind, receive divine touch of God and be relieved in the name of Jesus.

Lord strengthen me in my inner mind with Your fire and Your power in the name of Jesus.

I cast down every evil imagination in my heart in the name of Jesus.

I bring into captivity every area of my thought life to the obedient of Christ in the name of Jesus.

Sting of fear and failure, release my mind in the name of Jesus.

Lord, preserve my mind with Your fire in the name of Jesus.

I uproot every hidden evil tree in my mind in the name of Jesus.

I bind and cast down the spirit of uncertainty in my mind and I render its activity null and void in my life in the name of Jesus.

Holy Ghost, occupy every area vacated by the spirit of uncertainty in my mind in the name of Jesus.

Lord, every damage that spirit of uncertainty has done in my life be repaired and restored in the name of Jesus.

I recover and possess every good thing lost to the uncertain in the name Jesus.

My mind, I command you to think right in the name of Jesus.

Lord, soak my mind with heavenly revelations.

I gather together every area of my mind that has been fragmented in the name of Jesus.

ABOUT THE AUTHOR

Joel Odunayo Daramola whom God raised from grass to grace, has pioneered many parishes in The Redeemed Christian Church of God.

Currently: As Assistance Provincial Pastor Admin in Lagos province 37.

A graduate of The Redeemed Christian Bible College (RCBC), School of Disciple (SOD) and Institute of Leadership.

He holds a B.A. (Ed) in Guidance and Counseling from the prestigious University of Lagos (UNILAG).

He is a teacher who is registered with the teacher's registration council of Nigeria (TRCN)

A trained R & A Engineer (thermodynamics) with over 30 years' experience.

He is the CEO, Ayo-Technical Services (ATS). & Vision Link For You and I.

He is the host of Power Service (a weekly breakthrough and deliverance service) for over two decades.

A prolific writer, author of many books; a respected Evangelist, a gifted prophet with vast insight into the word of God.

Publisher of the Monthly Journal: "VISION LINK" for more than 20 years.

He has the vision to challenge young people to actualize their potentials in life.

His mandate is to spread the word of God, raise disciples, and build them to maturity for the perfection of saints through God's empowerment.

A prolific speaker, dexterous writer and a leading voice in Ministry and Leadership circles,

He is sought as a Conference speaker across the globe. His ministry is in high demand by both denominational and non-denominational ministries alike as his ability to engage people with God's word and effective prayer

He is passionate about raising people who are thoroughly steeped in Kingdom values and very relevant in the Secular world.

He believes that Christians should be able to influence society with kingdom principles.

His fine blend of excellence and spirituality has made him stand out from the pack.

He believes God has a plan for everybody and that God can take the most unlikely and use him powerfully.

A Youth leader, an administrator, entrepreneur and motivational speaker with a global vision.

A motivational speaker for over two decades. He has organized seminars and conferences to inspire the Youths in schools and Church for Nation building, Vision discovery and career advancement. His fine blend of excellence and spirituality has made him stand out from the pack, he believes that God has a plan for everybody and that God can make use of anyone powerfully.

He has published many books; Sounds of the abundance of rain; At the darkest hour; Are you passing through? Destined for greatness but tied down among others.

He is happily married to Pastor (Mrs.) C.O. Daramola and their union is blessed with four Children: Power, Queen, Excellence and Great.

Emails: pastordara@yahoo.com & visionlinkdara1@gmail.com

Phone & WhatsApp +2348033275896.

Facebook: Joel Odunayo Daramola

Websites: www.visionlink4u.com

www.ingramcontent.com/pod-product-compliance
Lightning Source LLC
La Vergne TN
LVHW050335160826
845677LV00014B/3626